FESTIVALS OF THE WORLD
EGYPT

W
FRANKLIN WATTS
LONDON • SYDNEY

This edition first published in 2006 by
Franklin Watts
338 Euston Road
London
NW1 3BH

This edition is published for sale only in the
United Kingdom & Eire.

© Marshall Cavendish International (Asia) Pte Ltd 2006
Originated and designed by Marshall Cavendish
International (Asia) Pte Ltd
A member of Times Publishing Limited
Times Centre, 1 New Industrial Road
Singapore 536196

Written by: Elizabeth Berg
Edited by: Katharine Brown-Carpenter
Designed by: Sri Putri Julio
Picture research: Thomas Khoo and Joshua Ang

A CIP catalogue record for this book is available from
the British Library.

ISBN 0 7496 6774 5

Dewey Classification: 394.26962

Printed in Malaysia

CONTENTS

It's Festival Time . . .

Want to go for a boat ride on the Nile? You'll get your chance when we go out for the 'Smelling the Breeze' festival. We'll go on a picnic, too. Maybe a mummy will join us! Or maybe you'd rather stay up all night eating and dancing? Then come to Ramadan! Or we could play on the swings for Eid. Put on your new clothes and come along – it's holiday time in Egypt . . .

WHERE'S EGYPT?

E gypt is located in the north-east corner of Africa. Most of Egypt is covered by the Western Desert, part of the Sahara. The Nile River cuts through Egypt, flowing from its source in tropical

An Egyptian girl. Modern Egyptians are a mixture of many different peoples.

Africa to the Mediterranean Sea. For thousands of years, the yearly flooding of the Nile made the land on its banks very fertile. The Nile River made Egypt a rich country in ancient times.

Who are the Egyptians?

Ancient Egypt is the oldest civilisation in the world. All Western cultures have their roots in ancient Egypt. The **pharaohs** ruled Egypt for many thousands of years until they were conquered by invaders. Egypt then became a Christian nation. Much later, **Islam** swept over the region. Today, most Egyptians are Muslims, but there are also some Coptic Christians.

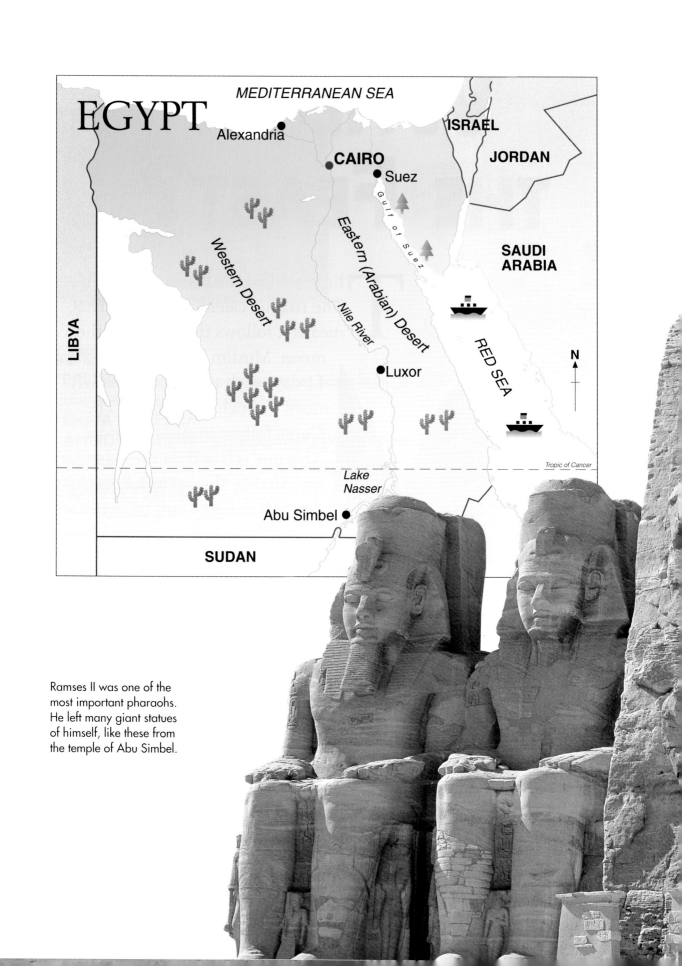

EGYPT

MEDITERRANEAN SEA

Alexandria

CAIRO

Suez

ISRAEL

JORDAN

Gulf of Suez

Western Desert

Eastern (Arabian) Desert

Nile River

LIBYA

SAUDI ARABIA

RED SEA

N

Luxor

Tropic of Cancer

Lake Nasser

Abu Simbel

SUDAN

Ramses II was one of the most important pharaohs. He left many giant statues of himself, like these from the temple of Abu Simbel.

During Ramadan, lanterns hang all around the streets. While they are lit, it is time to eat, drink and have fun.

Breaking the fast

The celebration starts every night with the iftar meal. Long into the night, Muslims continue feasting and talking with friends and family, listening to Arabic music and Islamic readings on the radio or going together to pray at the mosque. Restaurants and shops are open late, and the streets are full of people.

Singing traditional Arabic music, dancing and other entertainment are all part of the evening festivities.

Sweets are eaten before the iftar meal as a quick energy boost when breaking fast.

Muhammad's teachings

It is one of the laws set down in the **Qur'an** that Muslims should fast during the month of Ramadan. The Qur'an is the Muslim holy book. It not only tells Muslims about God, but it tells them about how they should live. The Prophet Muhammad received the Qur'an from the Angel Gabriel while meditating in a cave during the month of Ramadan. Muhammad could not read or write, but the angel made him recite the words that God had given. Muhammad memorised the entire Qur'an so he could tell the people what God had said. Later, his followers wrote down what he had said. Muhammad went out and told the people of Mecca in Saudi Arabia that there was only one god, called **Allah**, which means 'the God'. The religion he preached is called Islam, which means 'submission'. Today, there are Muslims on every continent of the world.

Think about this

Muslims believe in the same prophets as Christians do. In addition, they believe that the last prophet was Muhammad and that his revelation is the most perfect. They call Christians and Jews 'the people of the Book' because, like Muslims, they follow the Bible.

11

EID EL-FITR

I n times long past, on the evening of the 29th day of Ramadan, the chief judge would be escorted by a great procession to Mogattam Hill to look for the new moon. If he was able to see the moon, the announcement was made that the fasting month had ended. If he could not see it, Ramadan would continue for another day. Today, an observatory is used to look for the new moon. The announcement is made on the radio when the moon is sighted. If it is a cloudy night, reports may be sent from other Muslim countries to let people know that the fasting month is over. Then people know that the next day will be Eid el-Fitr and their fast is finished.

The women of the family usually get together to prepare special foods for Eid. These women are making *kahk*, a traditional bread served for Eid.

Dressing up

Before Eid comes, people paint and decorate their house, buy gifts and send greeting cards to neighbours, friends and relatives. On the day of the festival, they wake up early and put on their best clothes. All the children get new clothes for Eid. Then all the men and boys go to the mosque to pray. Women and girls either go to the mosque or stay at home to prepare the big feast.

Everyone goes to special Eid prayers. These are often held outside in parks or city squares.

Mohammad Ali Mosque in Cairo lit up for the holidays.

A day to have fun

Families go out to the park or go sailing on the Nile for Eid.

After going to the mosque to pray, Muslims go out to the park or go sailing on the Nile. All around, you can hear people greeting each other with the words 'Eid Mubarak'. That means 'Happy Eid'. It is also a good time for family reunions and for visiting friends. People who live far away from their family always try to come home for the Eid holiday. It is a time to patch up any quarrels you may have had during the year and to spend time with the people you care about. Muslims also take time to think about others at this time of year. If they can afford it, they give money at the mosque. This money is given to the poor of the community so that they can also take part in the Eid festivities.

Think about this

There are really only two festivals for Muslims: Eid el-Fitr and Eid el-Adha. That's because Muslims are supposed to practise their faith every day, not just a few days of the year. In some countries, people also celebrate other important days.

Opposite: Children dressed up in their new clothes for the holiday.

EID EL-ADHA

The most important Islamic festival is Eid el-Adha, which means 'Feast of the Sacrifice'. That's because it celebrates a famous sacrifice. Do you know the story of Abraham? God told Ibrahim (that's what Muslims call him) to go to the mountain and sacrifice his son. Ibrahim obeyed God's command. Before he slit the boy's throat, though, he covered his eyes. When he uncovered them, he found that he had sacrificed a sheep instead. His son was alive.

Give everything for God

Celebrating Eid el-Adha reminds people that, like Ibrahim, they must be willing to make any sacrifice for God. To show their willingness to sacrifice their wealth and even their life for God, Muslims buy an animal and sacrifice it. In the days before the festival, the streets of Cairo fill with sheep. Afterwards, the owners give away one-third of the meat to friends, one-third to family and one-third to the poor. Then everyone celebrates the holiday with a big feast.

Eid el-Adha is also a time for children to have fun.

Take a trip

Eid el-Adha is also the time of year when Muslims fulfill an important obligation. Every Muslim who can visits Mecca once. This is called the *hajj*. People go on the hajj during Eid el-Adha. They visit the **Ka'ba**, the first building ever made for the worship of one god. Other rituals also celebrate important moments in Ibrahim's life. At hajj time, millions of Muslims from all over the world come together to worship Allah. It is one of the most important events in a Muslim's life.

The Ka'ba was built by Ibrahim. Here, the courtyard of the mosque is filled with pilgrims, who walk around the Ka'ba three times.

One Egyptian tradition is to paint a mural on the wall of your home after you have been on the hajj. Can you see the pilgrim dressed in white? How do you think this person travelled?

MOULID EL-NABI

Let's go to El-Hussein Square in Cairo. It's the 11th day of the month of Rabi el-Awal, the day when Muslims celebrate the birth of Muhammad, their prophet. Big tents are set up all around the square. Coloured lights are draped from the buildings, and the streets are aglow. You can hear holy men reciting the Qur'an and poems in praise of the Prophet. Let's go into one of the tents. Help yourself to some of the food they are serving. Soon, the great procession will begin, when musicians from the army lead all the religious groups, carrying their banners and singing praises to the Prophet, back to El-Hussein Square. This is Moulid el-Nabi, the Birthday of the Prophet.

Left: A Sufi dancer shows off his skill. At a moulid, you can hear music everywhere, and there are special performances all around.

Opposite: Musicians in a village zaffa procession on the back of a truck.

Think about this

There are moulids for everyone. Muslims celebrate important Islamic figures as well as holy men. Christians have one for the Virgin Mary and one for St. George. Jews celebrate the moulid of Abu Hasira. There are over 5,000 moulids every year!

Swings are set up in the streets during the moulid celebrations.

What happens at a moulid?

Moulid means 'birth'. It is a celebration of the birthday of an important religious person. A few days before, big tents are put up and the area is decorated with banners and lights. On the day of the moulid, there is a big *zaffa* procession with much music and celebration. The most fun part, though, is the evening entertainment. Markets are set up where you can buy sweets, toys, clothes and many other items. There are swings, merry-go-rounds and puppet shows. Maybe you'll even find a storyteller telling an exciting tale of adventure.

CHRISTMAS

Most Egyptians are Muslim, but not all. There is also a very old group of Christians called the Copts. They go back to the time before Islam came to Egypt. They have their own calendar and celebrate Christmas on 7 January instead of 25 December, as some Christians do. Copts fast during the day for a few weeks before Christmas. After a midnight church service, they go home to break their fast and children receive new clothes and gifts. Long ago, Muslims and Copts celebrated Christmas and many other holidays together. Today, Copts celebrate their festivals with church services.

Left: A night market lit up for the Christmas season.

Opposite: Copts making wreaths to decorate tombs at Christmas time.

CELEBRATING NATURE

On the day after Easter Sunday, all Egyptians celebrate one of their best-loved festivals, Sham el-Nessim. They get out of bed early in the morning and go outside. They take picnic lunches with them, and they spend the day in the park or boating on the Nile. They make sure to pack some salted fish, some kidney beans and some green onions. It is an old tradition to eat those foods on this special day. In fact, this tradition goes all the way back to the ancient Egyptians. Can you imagine the pharaohs taking along picnic lunches to celebrate the beginning of spring?

Sham el-Nessim

Sham el-Nessim means 'Smelling the Breeze'. There is an old saying in Egypt that 'he who sniffs the first spring zephyr [breeze] will have good health all year'. What better excuse for a picnic?

Sham el-Nessim is now just a day set aside to breathe in the fresh spring air. But a hundred years ago, it was a harvest festival. At that time, it was the biggest festival in Egypt!

The food is ready!
Come along for the picnic!

Have an onion

Many people smell an onion first thing when they wake up on the morning of Sham el-Nessim. They may also hang onions on the front door to protect their home. Egyptians have always thought onions are very good for your health. The ancient Egyptians drew them in tomb paintings. They believed onions could cure many illnesses.

A woman collects pigeon eggs. Eggs were a symbol of new life in ancient Egypt. That is where the tradition of colouring eggs began.

An ancient wall painting shows dancers and musicians. Festivals in ancient Egypt were celebrated with sacrifices, feasting, drinking and dancing.

Nilometers were built in many temples to measure how much the Nile waters had risen during the flood season.

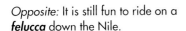

Think about this
Do you celebrate any festivals for the change of seasons? While some festivals only celebrate a season, others have a religious meaning, too. Can you think of any Christian holidays that also celebrate a season?

Opposite: It is still fun to ride on a *felucca* down the Nile.

Celebrating the Nile

The Nile River has always been the centre of Egyptian festivals. In ancient times, festivals often included a procession on the Nile. Today, going out on the Nile is still part of many festivals. And in August every year, there is a festival just to celebrate the Nile. In ancient times, the Egyptians took statues of the gods to the river in a big procession. They carried lamps on their boats and sang and danced. They asked the Nile to rise and gave offerings to the river. All night long, they feasted and celebrated, each person drinking from the waters of the Nile. Today, there is still a Nile festival but it is much smaller. A few years ago, Egypt constructed a huge dam and the Nile no longer floods every year. However, the Egyptians never forget their debt to the Nile.

An ancient painting shows a man boating on the Nile.

25

THINGS FOR YOU TO DO

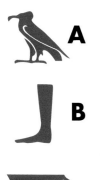
A

Would you like to celebrate a festival with the ancient Egyptians? Why not have a party for Sham el-Nessim and invite some mummies to come? But first you would have to send them an invitation. Of course, they would not understand if you wrote it in English. You will have to learn to write in **hieroglyphics**. What are hieroglyphics? They are signs that ancient Egyptians used to write things down. Want to try?

How to write in hieroglyphics

Sound out the word you want to write and find the hieroglyph that goes with each sound. Think about the sound and not the way the word is spelt in English. Now that you have the hieroglyphs, you have to put them together. They can be written in any direction. Just make sure that the animals and birds are facing towards the beginning of the word or sentence so the other person knows what direction to read. And you do not have to write them in a straight line. You can bunch them up so they look nice. Try writing your name. Experiment with different ways of writing it.

B

C,K

D

I,Y

F,V

G

H

CH

E

J

M

N

P

Q

L,R

S

T

O,U,W

SH

TH

Z

Make an invitation

Now it is time to write your invitation. Ancient Egyptians usually wrote important messages on a papyrus scroll. Papyrus was something like paper but it was made from the papyrus plant, which grows along the Nile. You can use paper – it is close enough. Take a long piece of paper and write your invitation. Make it look nice. You may want to add a little colour to the hieroglyphs. Then roll it up and tie it with a ribbon. Deliver it to the nearest mummy and get ready for your party.

Further information

www.stmarkcoccleveland.org/copticchurch.html – the history of the Coptic Christians
http://atschool.eduweb.co.uk/carolrb/islam/festivals.html – a simple introduction to Islam
www.touregypt.net/featurestories/festival.htm – more information about festivals in ancient Egypt
www.holidays.net/ramadan/story.htm – more detailed information about the month of Ramadan

Every effort has been made by the Publisher to ensure that these websites are suitable for children and contain no inappropriate or offensive material. However, because of the nature of the Internet, it is impossible to guarantee that the contents of these sites will not be altered. We strongly advise that Internet access is supervised by a responsible adult.

MAKE A BEADED COLLAR

T he pharaohs used to wear wide collars set with precious stones. You can dress up just like the pharaohs with your own beaded collar! Try it – you will look just like King Tut.

You will need:

1. A ruler
2. Two 12.5-cm strips of Velcro
3. A pencil
4. Scissors
5. Glue
6. Braid
7. Coloured beads
8. A large piece of felt

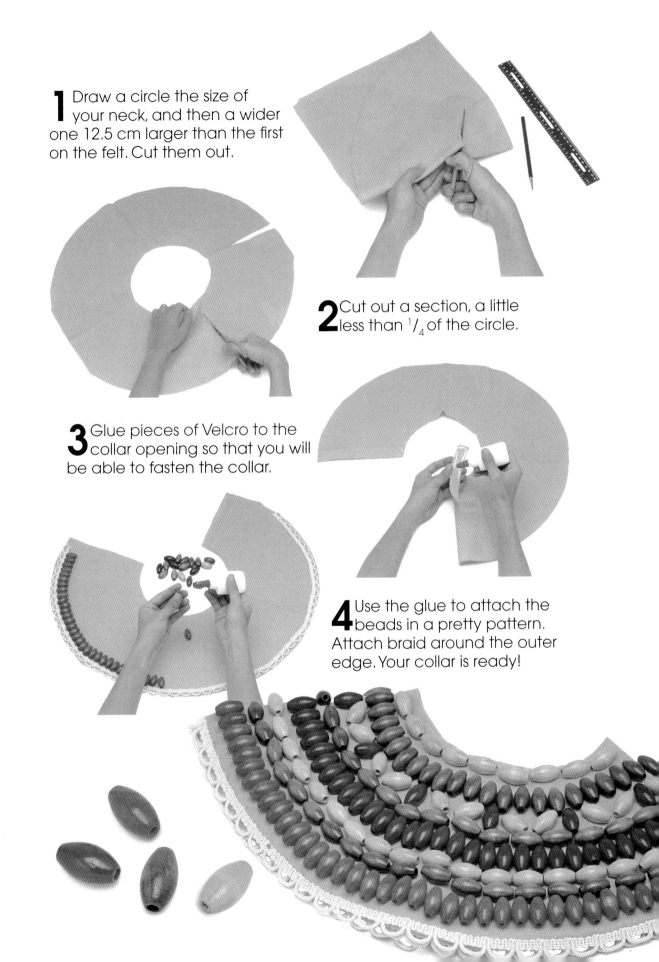

1 Draw a circle the size of your neck, and then a wider one 12.5 cm larger than the first on the felt. Cut them out.

2 Cut out a section, a little less than $\frac{1}{4}$ of the circle.

3 Glue pieces of Velcro to the collar opening so that you will be able to fasten the collar.

4 Use the glue to attach the beads in a pretty pattern. Attach braid around the outer edge. Your collar is ready!

MAKE GRANDMA'S NUT CAKE

Everyone has special sweet treats that they make for Eid el-Fitr. Here's one you could try (with a little help from a grown-up). But be warned – Egyptians like their desserts sweet. Are you ready for a really sweet festival treat?

You will need:

1. 100 g unsalted butter
2. 450 g sugar
3. 6 eggs
4. 340 g sifted flour
5. 3 teaspoons baking powder
6. 1 teaspoon ground cinnamon
7. $\frac{1}{2}$ teaspoon salt
8. 250 g chopped nuts
9. 240 ml water
10. A pinch of fenugreek
11. A wooden spoon
12. A measuring jug
13. Measuring cups
14. A saucepan
15. Measuring spoons
16. Mixing bowls
17. A sieve
18. A baking tray
19. An oven glove

1 Cream the butter and 190 g of sugar until the mixture is light and fluffy. Add the eggs one at a time, beating after each egg.

2 Sift together the flour, baking powder, cinnamon and salt. Pour the flour mixture into the egg mixture and mix well. Add the nuts.

3 Pour into a baking tray. It should be about 2.5 cm deep. Bake at 180° Celsius (gas mark 4) for 35 minutes. (Ask a grown-up to help you with this part.)

4 Combine the rest of the sugar, the water and the fenugreek in a saucepan. Ask an adult to help you cook it over low heat, stirring constantly, until the sugar dissolves. Then boil it for 3 minutes. Pour the syrup over the cake.

GLOSSARY

Allah, 11	The Muslim name for God.
Copts, 6	Members of the Egyptian Christian Church.
felucca, 25	A traditional Egyptian boat that is used on the Nile.
hajj, 17	A pilgrimage to Mecca that each Muslim should make.
hieroglyphics, 26	Alphabet that was used in ancient Egypt.
iftar, 8	The meal that breaks the fast during Ramadan.
Islam, 4	A religion that follows the teachings of the Prophet Muhammad.
Ka'ba, 17	The first building made for the worship of one god.
lunar, 6	Following the phases of the moon.
pharaohs, 4	The rulers of ancient Egypt.
Qur'an, 11	The Muslim holy book (sometimes spelled Koran).
sohour, 8	The morning meal before fasting during Ramadan.
zaffa, 19	A procession for a moulid.

INDEX